Nature's Children

GOLDFISH

by Robert Hirschfeld

GROLIER
EDUCATIONAL

FACTS IN BRIEF

Classification of the Goldfish

Class:	*Osteichthyes*
Order	*Cypriniformes*
Family:	*Cyprinidae* (carp)
Genus:	*Carassius* (freshwater fish)
Species:	*Carassius auratus*

World distribution: Originally native to China, goldfish were introduced to many other parts of the world, including North America and Europe.

Habitat: Home aquariums, ornamental ponds.

Distinctive physical characteristics: Domesticated goldfish are 1 to 4 inches long (2.5 to 10 centimeters); most commonly brassy orange or red in color. In the wild, goldfish grow up to 1 foot in length (30.5 centimeters) and revert to their original greenish-brown color.

Habits: Hearty eaters. Can live in many different environments.

Diet: Goldfish are omnivorous, feeding on small crustaceans and aquatic plants.

Library of Congress Cataloging-in-Publication Data

Hirschfeld, Robert. 1942-
    Goldfish / Robert Hirschfeld
        p.   cm. — (Nature's children)
    Includes index.
    Summary: Describes the physical characteristics, behavior,
habitats, and care of various types of goldfish.
    ISBN 0-7172-9069-7 (hardcover)
    1. Goldfish—Juvenile literature. [1. Goldfish.]   I. Title.
II. Series.
SF458.G6H57 1997
639.3'7484—dc21

97-2999
CIP
AC

This library reinforced edition was published in 1997 exclusively by:

Grolier Educational

Sherman Turnpike, Danbury, Connecticut 06816

Set ISBN 0-7172-7661-9
Goldfish ISBN 0-7172-9069-7

Contents

Goldfish are among the most popular pets in the world.

Along with cats and dogs, goldfish are among the most popular pets in the world. Easy to care for and fascinating to watch, goldfish come in many varieties. Some are rather plain looking, while others boast extraordinary color and beauty.

For more than a century, millions of people have brought pet goldfish home in little glass fishbowls. Unfortunately, most of those goldfish do not survive in such an unsuitable habitat. As a result, many owners have concluded that goldfish are delicate and hard to keep. This is not so.

In truth, goldfish are quite hardy and often live very long lives, even in difficult conditions. Many varieties, in fact, are so strong that they can even thrive outdoors in ponds or wading pools. It is no wonder that goldfish have been favored pets for hundreds of years.

Goldfish History

The Chinese are generally credited with being the first people to breed and keep pet goldfish. All of this took place before the year 1000 AD with a wild fish called the crucian carp. No one knows exactly why goldfish were so popular in China. But it is assumed that at least some of their popularity stemmed from their hardiness and bright golden color.

It was the Japanese, however, who took the hobby of goldfish breeding to new heights. Beginning in the 1500s they used selective breeding to create many of the colorful creatures we see in books and aquariums today.

The goldfish hobby spread to Europe around 1700. In 1876, the first goldfish were brought to the United States, and it was not long before Americans were fascinated by the graceful creatures. By 1900, goldfish farms were already producing millions of these pet fish in all different forms and colors for nationwide distribution.

Since then goldfish have risen and fallen in popularity several times. But in the end they remain one of everyone's favorite pets.

By the 1500s, Japanese fish fanciers were breeding exotic, beautiful fish.

A goldfish's torpedo-shaped body helps it move through the water.

Something Fishy

The shape of a fish and the structure of its body parts are perfectly suited to life in the water. Its streamlined, torpedo-shaped body, for example, helps a fish move through the water quickly and easily. Tail fins move the fish forward, while fins on the belly, sides, and back help it steer and turn.

Another part of a fish's swimming equipment is the swim bladder. When this organ fills with gas, the fish rises; when it empties, the fish moves downward.

Most fish also have a special armor to protect themselves from injury or attack. These colorless, platelike scales cover the fish's entire body.

Fish also have breathing equipment that lets them live in the water. In order to survive fish need oxygen to breathe, just as we do. But instead of lungs, fish breathe with gills. These allow fish to take oxygen from the water and transfer it into their bloodstreams.

Fish also are cold-blooded, which means that a fish's body temperature changes with the temperature of its surroundings. This, too, helps them survive even in cool water.

All Goldfish Are Not Alike

Fish fall into two main categories: freshwater fish (those found in rivers, lakes, and ponds) and saltwater, or marine, fish, which live in oceans or seas. All goldfish are freshwater fish.

There are about 125 breeds of goldfish. Many are golden in color, but some are black or a mix of other colors. Fancy, or exotic, goldfish often are highly unusual in appearance, with bulging eyes, double or triple fins, and a dazzling range of colors. Some of the rarest, most unusual breeds actually are considered quite ugly—especially those with peculiar head shapes.

It is useful to remember that the odder varieties of goldfish are more difficult to care for than the more common ones. But even exotic goldfish can live for quite a long time if they are properly cared for.

*These fish come in many colors
besides gold and orange.*

Choosing Goldfish

One of the best ways to purchase healthy goldfish is to find a pet store with a reputation for quality and cleanliness. Once there, buyers should look for fish that are active swimmers, with clear eyes and erect fins. Fish with clouded eyes may be blind, and droopy fins are a sign that a fish might be ill.

Buyers also should be on the lookout for dead fish. A few of these are normal in any pet store. But more than a few dead fish usually mean that there is a problem of some sort.

Buyers always should feel free to ask the store owner anything about the fish. If the owner seems reluctant or unable to answer questions, then it might be best to go to a different store.

In general, first-time buyers should avoid fancy breeds of goldfish. The more exotic breeds often are expensive and, just as important, usually need the care of experienced owners.

It also is wise to get only one variety of goldfish for each tank or aquarium. Some varieties are faster swimmers than others and may take all the food.

The Best Varieties for Beginners

For people new to goldfish, the best varieties to buy are ones that do not need careful handling. Single-tailed goldfish such as the common goldfish, the comet, and the shubunkin are all quite hardy and easy to care for.

The common goldfish is usually bright orange in color and has a short tail and a long, streamlined body. It is a very active fish that can live up to 10 years.

The comet is a variety that was developed in the United States during the late 1880s. Similar in appearance to the common goldfish, the comet's tail is longer and comes to a point.

Although their name makes them sound as if they might be rare or exotic, shubunkins are actually even hardier than the common and comet varieties. (The name comes from a Japanese word that means deep-red fish.) Extremely strong swimmers, they need an especially large tank. But with simple care, shubunkins can live up to 20 years.

*Most fancy goldfish are double-tailed,
with long, sweeping tailfins.*

Fancy That!

Most fancy goldfish are double-tailed, but some varieties have rounded rather than streamlined bodies. Fairly slow swimmers, round-bodied fish should be kept separate from faster varieties. This will prevent conflict during feeding, when the slower, round-bodied fish have a hard time competing for food.

The fantail variety is one of the most popular round-bodied goldfish. It is named for the wide, double tailfins that stream out in the shape of a fan. Bright orange or white in color, a full-size fantail is about four inches (10 centimeters) in body length with a four-inch (10-centimeter) tail. Extremely hardy, it can live from five to ten years. Fantails are easy to care for in either a regular tank or an outdoor pond.

Another fancy goldfish, the oranda, needs a steady water temperature of about 65° Fahrenheit (18° Celsius). As a result, it usually is kept indoors. Orange or red in color, the oranda has an odd, bumpy head covering that looks like a red cauliflower!

The telescope variety is one of the more unusual fancy goldfish. It has terrible eyesight because its eyes stick straight out from the sides of its head!

Round-bodied goldfish are slower, poorer swimmers than the slim varieties.

Beware the Poorest Swimmers!

Some varieties of round-bodied goldfish have no back, or dorsal, fins, making them the poorest swimmers among goldfish. They need expert care.

The lionhead (which also is called the tomatohead) is one of the most striking of these fish. It gets its name—as well as a lot of attention—from the rounded mane that grows, like a big blister, on its head. Gold or sometimes yellow in color, the lionhead has a short, heavy body and can grow to five inches (12.5 centimeters) in length.

Pompoms also have strange-looking heads, with two rounded "flowers" growing from their noses! Another exotic, the brocaded goldfish, has striking color patterns that make the fish look like a beautiful piece of fabric.

Strange-looking eyes are common among the exotic round-bodied fish. Celestials, for example, have eyes that stick out and point straight up—so much that these goldfish can't even see directly in front of themselves!

*First-time owners probably should avoid
exotic, hard-to-care for goldfish.*

Getting Started

Caring for any kind of pet is a big commitment. So before taking on the responsibility of a goldfish aquarium, a future owner should find out the cost and care involved. Most pet stores sell inexpensive owner's manuals about goldfish. Reading one of these will let the future owner know exactly what he or she is in for.

A good aquarium or pet store will have many different breeds of goldfish. It also will have all the food and equipment needed to raise the fish and keep them healthy. The people who work in the store should be able to give good advice about which fish to buy and what supplies will be needed. They also can provide information about how many fish to start with, which variety to buy, and how to set up an aquarium tank.

The most important thing, at this point, is for future owners to ask questions—and to be honest. If a person does not have a lot of time to put into the care and maintenance of the fish, he or she should admit it from the beginning. Choosing fish that need less care is far better than getting ones that need care and don't get it.

No Fishbowls, Please

Before a new owner buys any fish, the homes for those fish have to be purchased and set up. The first thing to consider is the size and shape of the fish's home.

Goldfish often are displayed in small, round fish bowls. But these generally are too small to use as long-term homes. In the first place they do not have enough surface area—the amount of water in contact with air—to provide goldfish with the oxygen they need. Nor do they have enough space for active or fast-moving varieties to swim.

Surprisingly, goldfish need a lot of room—something people should remember when they buy or set up a home for their pets. Goldfish grow rapidly and can quickly become too big for a small tank. Also, goldfish are big eaters and produce a lot of waste. In a small tank, this can be a problem, too.

For this reason, experts suggest that four goldfish need at least a 20-gallon (76-liter) tank. A tank like this might seem too big at first, and it may cost a little bit more. But in the long run, it will make for happier, healthier fish.

Goldfish need a lot of room, as well as other equipment, in order to do well.

Equipping a Goldfish Tank

Although goldfish have only a few basic needs, more than just a good-size tank is necessary. As with many pets, proper care of goldfish requires investing in the proper equipment.

An aquarium, for example, should always have a cover that fits over the top of the tank. Made of glass or plastic, it prevents fish from leaping out of the tank.

The tank also will need a light. Most aquarium lights are fitted to the exact size of the tank. The best ones use fluorescent bulbs; incandescent bulbs can heat up the water and make it uncomfortable for the fish.

A filter is standard tank equipment as well, and its job is to keep the water clean. Many kinds are available, so owners should inquire at a pet store about which filter will work best with a particular tank or tank size.

Most aquariums also have machines, called aerators, that pump air bubbles into the water. Aerators add more oxygen to the water and help get rid of carbon dioxide.

Finally, there is a heater. Goldfish do well in a temperature range of 46° to 64° Fahrenheit (8° to 18° Celsius), so heaters are not normally required. However, a pet store owner can help you decide if there is a special reason to use a heater in a particular tank.

Aerators send off bubbles that provide extra
oxygen for an aquarium.

Making a Tank a Home

When the tank comes home, it will need a strong table or stand. A 20-gallon (76-liter) tank filled with water will weigh almost 200 pounds (90 kilograms), so it is best to check the stand for strength before the tank goes on it.

The tank and stand should then be placed where they will get daylight but not direct sunlight. Sunlight can cause the water temperature to rise which, in turn, can lower the amount of oxygen. Sunlight also can speed up the growth of tiny plants called algae. A small amount of algae growth is a good thing for a goldfish tank. But too much clouds the water and dirties the walls of the tank.

Most owners cover the tank's bottom with gravel, which can be bought at a pet or aquarium store. For a 20-gallon tank (76-liter), 40 pounds (18 kilograms) of gravel are needed. It is important to make sure that no germs or traces of dangerous chemicals go into the tank. For this reason, the gravel should be put into a pail and washed thoroughly before it is put into the aquarium.

Goldfish not only need space; they also need protection from curious kittens!

Adding Water to the Tank

After the gravel is put into the tank, water can be added. (Spring water is best since it does not have added chemicals such as chlorine and fluoride.) To keep from churning up the gravel, the water can be gently poured into a bowl placed in the bottom of the tank.

Once the tank is filled with water, plants are put in. Pet stores carry both real plants—which goldfish like to nibble—and artificial ones. Plants are simply pushed, root end first, into the gravel.

Finally, the filter and aerator are added—as well as any decorations or ornaments that are wanted. The directions for how to put in the filter and aerator should be followed carefully. Then the filter and aerator can be turned on.

The goldfish should not be put into a tank for about 48 hours. This allows time for the water to be filtered and to be tested for mineral and acid levels. (Water that has too many minerals or that is too acidic or alkaline is unhealthy for the fish.) Most pet stores carry simple kits to test and correct aquarium water for these and other water problems. This waiting period also allows time for chemicals to evaporate from the water.

Bulging eyes, strange-looking heads, and long, drooping tail fins are traits of some exotic goldfish.

Putting Goldfish in the Tank

Although goldfish are hardy creatures, care should be taken when they are brought home from the pet store. Paying attention to a few simple details will help the fish adjust to their new environment quickly and safely.

Goldfish usually are brought home from pet stores in plastic bags filled with water from their old tanks. It is not a good practice to simply dump the fish into the new aquarium tank. That is because going directly from one water temperature to another might shock the fish's system.

Instead, the unopened bags of goldfish should be allowed to float in the tank for 15 minutes or so. This lets the temperature of the water in the bag become equal with the water temperature in the tank.

Next, owners should add some tank water to the plastic bag, giving the fish a chance to adjust to the new water. The fish should be left alone for another 15 minutes. Then, finally, the bag should be gently opened, allowing the fish to swim out into the new home.

Most goldfish leave the pet store in a plastic bag.

28

Feeding Goldfish

Goldfish have big appetites—too big for their own good! Because of this, owners should pay attention to exactly when and how much their pets are fed.

Pet goldfish should be fed twice a day, morning and night, on a regular schedule. And they should get only as much food as they can eat in about five minutes.

Goldfish enjoy a variety of foods, and a variety definitely is good for them. The most common goldfish food is dried, and it comes in the form of little flakes. It is a good idea to put this dried food in a container and presoak it with tank water before feeding it to the fish.

Pet stores have frozen and freeze-dried foods, such as insects and shrimp, that goldfish love. Most pet or aquarium stores also carry live goldfish food—tiny worms, insects, and so on. Goldfish will even eat shredded cooked vegetables or raw hamburger that is chopped or grated. But food meant for other kinds of fish should not be given to goldfish.

Even the most exotic goldfish enjoys a good meal—twice a day.

Daily Care of Goldfish

To make sure that their fish stay healthy, owners must carry out certain tasks on a regular basis. Some tasks are required periodically. Others should be done every day.

Because fish develop regular habits, they ought to be fed at the same times each day. Ideally this means one feeding in the morning and another at night.

As strange as it may sound, fish do sleep, and they sleep better with the light off. So the tank light should be on during the day and off at night.

In addition, the filter and aerator should be examined each day to be sure both are working properly. At the same time, the water temperature should be checked with a thermometer to make sure it is within a safe range for the fish.

When owners go on vacation for a week or so, it is not necessary to have someone in to feed the fish. If the fish are healthy and fit, they will do quite well without food for this period of time. For longer vacations, though, owners should try to find another knowledgeable fish keeper to tend to their fish. If the only available pet sitter is inexperienced, however, food should be left in small packets to avoid overfeeding. Underfeeding will not hurt the fish; overfeeding will.

Some goldfish are downright strange looking.

Weekly Care

Beyond daily care, there are certain jobs that should be taken care of once each week. Most are simple and should not take much time.

For example, once a week the goldfish should be checked for signs of illness. If the fish are not lively or are not swimming upright, or if they have swollen bodies or cloudy eyes, they may need medical attention.

Another weekly chore is to remove any parts of live plants that have turned brown. At the same time, bits of food, plants, and waste matter should be removed from the gravel. Fish fanciers call all of this stuff mulm, and pet stores sell special machines that make cleaning up mulm an easy job.

Finally, any water that has evaporated from the tank should be replaced. Normally, this involves about two gallons (7.6 liters) of water a week for a 20-gallon (76-liter) tank. Once again, however, water for a fish tank never should come straight from the tap. Instead, keep water handy in one- or five-gallon (3.8-liter or 19-liter) containers. It should "age" for several days before being added to the tank.

Even goldfish get the blues sometimes.

*It takes many generations of selective breeding
to create goldfish with these unusual qualities.*

Once-in-a-While Care

There are some chores that fish owners do not even have to do each week. These are once-in-a-while jobs, but they should not be forgotten.

Once a month, the sides of the aquarium should be scraped to prevent algae from taking over the tank. Pet or aquarium stores sell special tools for this purpose. At the same time, dirt should be cleaned from the filter and aerator as well as any ornaments in the tank. The water should be tested for acidity and mineral content on a monthly basis as well.

Every three months, the filter should be rinsed out or replaced. This will make sure that the filter keeps the water as clean and pure as possible.

Finally the tank should be emptied, cleaned, and refilled every six months. The gravel should be thoroughly washed and the water completely replaced at this time. The fish should get a temporary home in clean water while all this is going on.

All this activity might seem like a lot to do. But it actually ends up taking owners just a few hours each year—not a lot of time to spend on a pet.

Parasites and Fungi

Goldfish can become infested with parasites or fungi. Both of these are organisms that live off other creatures. These creatures, called hosts, provide the parasites and fungi with all or most of the nourishment they need. Both organisms can be harmful to goldfish, and an infested fish may spread the organisms to other fish in the tank. It is best to remove the fish from the tank as soon as possible and place them in a separate "hospital" tank.

On goldfish a fungus looks like a slimy or cottony patch of white. Parasites, however, come in many forms and varieties. Tiny disclike parasites called fish lice can fasten themselves to a fish's body. Other parasites, called anchor worms, may burrow under the fish's scales, while tiny parasites called flukes invade a fish's gills and make them red and swollen.

Owners should contact a vet or an aquarium expert whenever they see signs of either parasites or fungi. Pet stores have medications that work well. In general, all the fish in a tank should be treated, not just the individual fish. In that way, even if that one fish cannot be saved, its tank-mates might be able to be treated successfully.

Some of the strange-looking goldfish are especially hard to examine, but they still must be checked for parasites and fungi.

Other Health Problems

Parasites and fungi are not the only health problems fish can suffer. For example, fish can become constipated or get indigestion from food that disagrees with them.

Dry food, in particular, seems to trouble some varieties of goldfish, including the beautiful veiltail, which is slimmer than a fantail and has a long, flowing tail.

Another sign of a food problem is a fish that is swollen and lying at the bottom of the tank. Fish like these need a radical change in their diets. They should be placed in a hospital tank and not be fed for a few days. If they become active again, they can be fed freeze-dried food for a week and returned to their normal home. A permanent change in their diet is probably called for.

A fish that is swimming on its side or upside down probably has a swim bladder problem, something that is also caused by eating the wrong food. Special medicated food, sold by pet or aquarium stores, may help.

Goldfish also can develop tumors, which look like lumps on their bodies. Most tumors can be removed quite safely and simply by a vet.

Owners should make sure that fish are not sluggish or droopy-finned.

Keeping Goldfish Outdoors

Goldfish that can adjust to changing temperatures can thrive in an outdoor pond. Goldfish that are well suited for life outdoors include the common goldfish, the comet, and the fantail varieties.

The Japanese koi is the front-runner of outdoor pond and water garden fish. Unlike the common goldfish, the koi have barbels, or whiskerlike feelers. And they sometimes live as long as 60 years!

An outdoor goldfish pond should have exposure to both sun and shade. A pond should be no more than four feet (1.2 meters) deep, but, like indoor tanks, it should not be overcrowded. This is especially important because pond fish often grow much bigger than aquarium fish. Some even reach lengths of 18 inches (45 centimeters).

In cold-weather regions outdoor goldfish usually are removed from their ponds before winter sets in. They are then brought inside to warm, indoor aquariums.

Owners of fish ponds should be aware that many animals, especially birds and cats, are fish-eaters. For them, the owner's beautiful display of fish may end up being a snack bar!

Breeding Goldfish

Owners who wish to breed goldfish need proper equipment, including a second tank. This breeding (or spawning) tank should have live water plants around the sides, leaving the middle area clear. Special food is necessary for both adult and baby fish. Later, the offspring will need another tank of their very own.

Female goldfish can spawn, or lay eggs, for the first time when they are a year old. The spawning season takes place in spring or summer.

For a few months before breeding, the fish should be placed in cool water, a little over 50° Fahrenheit (10° Celsius). During this time, they will need less food, usually no more than what they can eat in three minutes per feeding. Food rich in carbohydrates— flake food, bread crumbs, and bits of pasta—are best.

At breeding time, the tank water should be warmed to about 67° Fahrenheit (20° Celsius). The adult male and female fish that will be breeding need more food—as much as they can eat in six minutes. They should be fed foods rich in protein, such as egg, beef, brine shrimp, and worms.

The Mating Game

At breeding time, owners should prepare the separate breeding tank and put an adult male and an adult female goldfish into it. Telling a female from a male can be difficult, but, in general, a female looks rounder because she is carrying eggs. A male develops tiny growths like pimples around his gills.

The female rubs herself against the plants in the tank and sprays out her eggs, which are tinier than sugar grains. The eggs quickly soak up water and swell.

The male then sprays what is called melt near the eggs. The melt contains the sperm that fertilizes the eggs.

Once they are fertilized, the eggs will either sink to the bottom of the tank or stick to the surface of the leaves. Then both adult fish should be put back in their regular tank to keep them from eating the eggs.

Breeding goldfish gives owners a wonderful supply of new and interesting fish.

Bringing Up Babies

The water temperature in the tank containing the eggs should be about 70° Fahrenheit (21° Celsius). If everything goes right, the eggs will begin to hatch in about five days. Then, one by one, they will hatch for the next several days.

For about two days after hatching, the new fish (called fry) remain attached to plants or to the tank. During this time they live off food stored in the egg.

The fry grow quickly. Once they start moving, the fish must be fed. Fry food can be bought at pet or aquarium stores. The larger fry should be separated from the smaller ones, which might otherwise be eaten.

After two weeks, the babies need a different diet. The larva of tiny animals called daphnia are available in pet stores and are an excellent source of food.

An adult fish may produce up to 25 baby fish, but only the healthy ones will survive. During the next two months, the smallest ones and those with defects such as missing fins or eyes will most likely die. But at the end of that time, owners will have healthy new goldfish.

Words to Know

Aerator   A machine to pump air into a tank, adding oxygen to the water.

Algae   Tiny plants that grow in water.

Barbels   Whiskerlike feelers.

Dorsal fin   The fin on a fish's back.

Fins   Thin, flat extensions of a fish's body, used for moving through and balancing in the water.

Fluke   A fish parasite.

Fry   Baby fish.

Fungus   A group of plants that obtain their nourishment from other plants and animals or from decaying plants and animals.

Gills   The breathing organs of fish.

Habitat   The natural environment in which a plant or animal lives.

Melt   The liquid given off by male fish to fertilize eggs.

Mulm   Bits of food, plants, and fish waste.

Scales   Platelike parts forming the outer covering of fish.

Spawn   To lay eggs.

Swim bladder   A balloonlike, gas-filled sac in a fish's abdomen. Fish inflate it to rise in the water, and deflate it to sink.

INDEX

Cover Photo: D. DeMello (Wildlife Conservation Society)
Photo Credits: Norvia Behling (Behling & Johnson Photography), page 25; Richard T. Bryant, page 8; D. DeMello (Wildlife Conservation Society), pages 14, 27, 45; Robert W. Ginn (Unicorn Stock Photos), page 29; Shirley Haley (Top Shots), page 21; Wernher Krutein (Photovault), pages 7, 11, 16, 18, 23, 31, 33, 35, 36, 39, 41; SuperStock, Inc., page 4.